GW00383014

THE
LITTLE EXOTIC VEGETABLE BOOK

Rosamond Richardson

PIATKUS

© 1987 Judy Piatkus (Publishers) Limited

First published in 1987
by Judy Piatkus (Publishers) Limited,
5 Windmill Street, London W1

British Library Cataloguing in Publication Data
Richardson, Rosamond
The little exotic vegetable book
1. Cookery (Vegetables)
I. Title
641.6'5   TX801

ISBN 0-86188-586-4

Drawings by Linda Broad
Designed by Susan Ryall
Cover illustrated by Lynne Robinson

Phototypeset in Linotron Plantin by
Phoenix Photosetting, Chatham
Printed and bound in Great Britain by
The Bath Press, Avon

CONTENTS

INTRODUCTION

Suddenly the world seems to have become smaller. Our supermarket shelves are crammed with tropical produce quite unfamiliar to our western eyes, all thanks to super-speed travel and ingenious quick-freezing techniques. High-powered marketing has begun to familiarise us with an eddoe, a mooli, a chayote and an amazing range of all shapes and sizes of squashes. Cans of bamboo shoots and lotus root are no longer the domain of the specialist oriental shop. How intriguing they all are, these exotic tropical vegetables. But as for integrating them into our western cuisine and introducing them to our tables – well, that's surely another matter altogether.

This little book is designed to guide you through this new experience of taste and texture and to assure you that, strange and mysterious as some of these vegetables may seem, they are far from difficult to prepare and cook, and their delicate flavours can add an indefinable quality to dishes prepared with them.

This collection of exotic 'vegetables' includes flower buds (globe artichoke), seed pods (okra and mange-tout), roots (sweet potato, salsify), stems (fennel and kohl rabi), shoots (bamboo shoots and asparagus), fruits (bell peppers and chayote), and leaves (pak choi and lambs' lettuce). All parts of the plant are here!

But not all of them are tropical produce, or necessarily 'exotic' – except perhaps in price! Artichokes and asparagus, fennel and chicory have become familiar to us over the past decade or so. Nonetheless they are now more widely available than ever before, and are imported from different growing areas around the world so that they are available throughout the year. So these four, along with the aubergine, the pepper family and celeriac, are included with their more exotic counterparts: bamboo shoots, plantain and waterchestnut.

A feast for the eyes and a feast for the palate! This little book reveals how this newly acquired treasure trove can transform your table with tropical tastes and gastronomic glamour.

'Ambassadors cropped up like hay
Prime ministers and such as they
Grew like asparagus in May
And dukes were two a penny.'
W.S. Gilbert, *The Gondoliers*

ASPARAGUS
Asparagus officinalis

The ancient Egyptians grew asparagus, and from earliest times it has been cultivated as a garden vegetable. The Greeks introduced it to southern Italy, where it gained enormous popularity with the Romans. They liked the thick, white variety, and Pliny mentions a species grown near Ravenna of which three heads weighed 1 lb! A Venetian writer, Giacomo Castelvento, shows that even by the 17th century it had not declined in fashion: 'In fields where they once grew corn and flax, they now raise asparagus.'

Demand for asparagus spread into France in the 16th century when it was introduced by La Quintinie, gardener to Louis XIV. He planted asparagus beds in order to cater for the taste of his monarch all the year round. By 1670 forced asparagus was finding its way on to the London markets, where it remains to this day a luxury item. Its nickname 'Sparrowgrass' lingers; in the trade it is still called 'grass'.

Asparagus has been found to have many uses in

folk medicine. It is strongly diuretic and was used for sluggish kidneys, and for liver and bladder complaints. It was a treatment for dropsy and, as it was also found to calm palpitations, was prescribed for heart conditions. It contains asparagine, an amino acid essential for growth and the division and regeneration of body cells. One French herbalist claimed that it alleviates stress and was beneficial for intellectuals! Culpeper said, 'Boiled with wine, and taken, is good to clear the sight, and being held in the mouth easeth the toothache.'

There are more than 100 species of asparagus which grow in temperate regions of Europe and the US. There are three main types on the market: the French, green asparagus, the purple Italian variety, and the thick white asparagus so loved by Germans and Americans. Small thin asparagus is sold as 'sprue', and its excellent flavour makes a delicious soup. The English season is at its height in May and June, and all asparagus is best eaten as fresh as possible, soon after it is cut. Asparagus has a high water content, 18 calories per 100g, 54% nitrogen, 3.5% protein, some mineral salts and vitamins A and C.

Choose tender, crisp stalks which are not woody at the base, and cook them tied in bundles in a tall thin pan with a tight fitting lid. The lower stems should stand in the boiling water, while the tips cook in the steam for about 10 minutes until tender. Asparagus is delightful on its own, hot or cold, with melted butter or sauce tartare. It makes a wonderful soup, is delicious in egg dishes and goes very well with parmesan cheese.

Asparagus Soufflé-Omelette

A soufflé-omelette is always impressive, yet it is made in minutes and just needs a salad and fresh granary bread to turn it into a wonderful meal.

8 oz (250 g) fresh asparagus
3 eggs, separated
salt and pepper
3 tablespoons thick cream
butter
1 tablespoon grated parmesan cheese

Trim any woody parts off the bottom of the asparagus and tie into a neat bundle. Stand in boiling water to about half way up the stalks and cover with a lid so that the tips steam. When they are tender, which will take about 10 minutes, depending on the type of asparagus, remove from the water and cut into 1 inch (2.5 cm) lengths.

Beat the egg yolks thoroughly and season with a little salt and pepper. Mix in the cream, then fold in the asparagus pieces. Then beat the whites until very stiff, and fold into the yolk base.

Melt a little butter in a heavy pan, pour in the mixture and put over a moderate heat until it begins to puff up. As it starts to set at the bottom, sprinkle the parmesan over the top and put under a moderate grill for a minute or two until the soufflé cooks through and begins to brown on top. Cut it in half and serve immediately.

For 2

AUBERGINE
Solanum melongeria, var. *esculentum*

The aubergine, also widely known as eggplant, has a large number of local names which reflect its folklore. It is 'Apple of Love', 'Garden Egg', 'Jew's Apple', 'Raging Apple', 'Widow's Comforter' (*Solanum* comes from the Latin 'to comfort'), and 'Mad Apple' because it was believed to cure insanity. Its Indian name, *brinjal*, was adopted for a while by the English in colonial times. Its original Sanskrit name has the meaning 'vegetable of the wind-disorder kind', and the aubergine was used by those embarrassed by excess wind in their systems!

The aubergine is a native of tropical Asia and probably India. The Arabs were responsible for introducing it into Spain during the Dark Ages, and the Spaniards later took it with them to the New World. It was introduced into England around 1597, but was still a rarity by the late 19th century, as the *Treasury of Botany* records: 'Aubergines or brinjals, which are highly esteemed in France, may occasionally be met with in Covent Garden market.' They were used in Hindu herbal medicine as a treatment for diabetes, and the *Kama Sutra* prescribes them in a concoction for 'enlarging the male organ for a period of one moon'.

Aubergines contain a bitter constituent which irritates the mucous membrane of the alimentary canal, so this is usually removed by salting aubergine slices and 'sweating' the bitterness out before cooking.

With a 93% water content, aubergines contain little nutritional value: 2.5 g dietary fibre to every 100 g, 14 calories and tiny amounts of mineral salts and vitamin C. They belong to the same family as potatoes, peppers and tobacco, and are exported nowadays from Spain and Italy, Israel and Holland, the West Indies and West Africa. Although widely available throughout the year, they are at their best in August and September and less bitter varieties are now being bred. The flesh should be creamy white and spongy, the skin a shiny purple and unblemished. They should feel firm and heavy, weighing on average about 12 oz (350 g), and will store for up to one week in the refrigerator.

Aubergines can be baked whole and the flesh scooped out for use in vegetable pâtés and soufflés. Or they can be sliced, sprinkled with salt and 'sweated' for 30 minutes so that they absorb less oil in cooking. Fried in oil or batter, they make a delicious side vegetable, and are an integral part of ratatouille and moussaka. Aubergines are excellent stuffed or baked *au gratin*, and in curries.

POOR MAN'S CAVIAR

This tasty purée of aubergines, well-flavoured with garlic and lemon juice, makes a fabulous starter. It is rich and satisfying food, with unusual resonances of Middle Eastern cuisine.

3 medium aubergines
2–3 large cloves of garlic, crushed
1/4 pint (150 ml) olive oil
juice of 1 lemon
3 tablespoons chopped parsley
sea salt

Bake the aubergines in their skins for about 40 minutes in a preheated oven at 350°F/180°C/Gas 4. Cool, then remove the pulp from the skins and purée it with the garlic, olive oil and lemon juice. Stir in the chopped parsley and season to taste with sea salt. Put into a pretty dish and refrigerate until well-chilled. Serve with warm pitta bread and a tomato and onion salad to pass around.

For 6

BABY SWEETCORN
Zea mays

Sweetcorn is American in origin, a native of Mexico, and it has been cultivated in the Americas for 3,000 years. It was the only cereal crop of the Aztec, Maya and Inca civilisations and a staple food of the North American Indians – hence its common name of 'Indian Corn'. It was brought to Europe by Columbus and is now grown world-wide. Corn oil, corn syrup, cornbread and cornflakes are all made from sweetcorn, and Bourbon is the product of fermented corn.

Baby sweetcorn are the very young, delicate ears of corn harvested when still tiny, about 2 inches (5 cm) long, and tender enough to eat whole. They are exported to the UK principally from Thailand and Kenya, and are available fresh from December to June. It is also possible to buy them frozen or canned.

Sweetcorn is a good source of starch, contains some minerals, vitamins A and C, and has 127 calories per 100 g. Eaten either whole or sliced, baby sweetcorn needs only very light cooking – a few minutes either steaming, stir-frying or boiling. Good ones are a bright, clear yellow and have a sweet flavour which is delicious with crab, chicken and prawns, and excellent in soups. It is also a worthy vegetable in its own right, tossed in a little melted butter. It gives a delectable crunch to a salad and is a tasty addition to Chinese stir-fried vegetables.

In 1766 Benjamin Franklin said, 'Indian corn, take it for all in all, is one of the most wholesome and agreeable grains in the world – Johnny and hoecake hot from the fire is better than a Yorkshire muffin.'

BAMBOO SHOOTS
Bambusa vulgaris

The bamboo is one of a large species of woody-stemmed grasses or reeds which grows in the tropics. It was given the name 'bambusa' when it arrived in Europe in the 16th century from the Far East. The spiky young shoots are dug just before they appear above the ground and are eaten fresh in China, Indo-China, India and Japan, rather like giant asparagus spears. They vary from 6–12 inches (15–30 cm) long, and up to 4 inches (10 cm) in diameter, are conical shaped and white. They are appetisingly crisp with a slightly acid flavour which goes particularly well with pork, stir-fried in a spicy sauce. They can be eaten either lightly cooked, or raw in a crunchy salad, and the Japanese have a traditional recipe for tender bamboo shoots in sake vinegar. The pith is very sweet, and in its countries of origin a syrup is made from it which is highly prized.

Sold fresh in oriental markets, bamboo shoots are only available canned in Europe, where they are sold as a luxury item. Once opened, put any excess bamboo shoots into a glass of fresh water, where they will keep in the fridge for several days. If they have acquired a tinny taste, blanch them briefly before using.

Bamboo shoots are lovely in chop suey, and go especially well with mushrooms, sliced and lightly cooked in butter with herbs. Try slicing them into soups for their crisp texture, or adding them to a *gratin* of French beans. A dish of lightly stir-fried mange-tout with slices of bamboo shoots makes an elegant and exotic side vegetable.

BREADFRUIT
Artocarpus communis

A native of the Pacific islands, breadfruit is associated with the Mutiny on the Bounty in 1787, when Captain Bligh was commissioned by the British government to take breadfruit plants from Tahiti to British planters in Jamaica. This large tree is now established in most parts of the tropics, but is not widely popular outside south east Asia and the Pacific. Also known as 'God's Jack', 'Breadnut', and 'Captain Bligh', it is a large, round fruit up to 8 inches (20 cm) in diameter and weighing up to 10 lb (4.5 kg). The flesh is yellow when ripe, and the skin, which is thick and warty, is a mottled brown and gold. The pulp is slightly sweet, moist and chewy, with a bread-like aroma; it is green until ripe, when it turns yellow. The fruits are borne in twos and threes at the end of the branches of a large tree, which can grow to a height of 90 feet (27.5 m).

Breadfruit is either baked whole or peeled and cut into chunks for casseroles and curries, in much the same way as potatoes. It goes well with tuna fish, or in cheese dishes, and can be filled with savoury stuffings. Cut into thin slices it can be fried like crisps, or roasted with a joint of meat. It also makes a substantial side vegetable when boiled until tender and served in a tasty sauce.

The chief nutritive value of the breadfruit lies in its high starch content, and it is a cheap source of bulk for the local areas in which it is a staple food. They say that two or three breadfruit trees produce enough food for one man for a whole year! The breadfruit contains 90 calories per 100 g and reasonable amounts of vitamins B and C. It is also available canned in brine.

CAPSICUM
Capsicum spp.

The capsicum is native to South America and is related to the potato, aubergine, tomato and tobacco. It is a species of about 50 varieties, which vary in size from the tiny, hot chilli to large, sweet 'bell' peppers. They come in many colours – green, red, yellow, ivory and purple. Cayenne pepper comes from the African Pepper, paprika from the Hungarian Sweet or Pimento Pepper, and chilli powder is a ground mixture of *C. frutescens* and other hot spices. The sweet bell pepper that we know as a vegetable rather than a spice is *C. anuum*.

First cultivated 7,000 years ago in Peru, capsicums were still being cultivated in South America when the Spanish explorers arrived in the 16th century. The Portuguese took them to the East

Indies, where they immediately became popular in oriental cookery, and the Spaniards brought them back to Europe, calling them 'pimienta', or peppers, because of their fiery taste. By 1618 dried peppers were available on the London markets, where they were known as Ginnie or Guinea peppers.

Peppers contain capsaicin, a stimulant to the circulation which raises the heartrate and causes sweating. They stimulate the digestion and are much used in heavy foods such as curries and spicy Mexican dishes, for this reason. They help to lower cholesterol, and have been used in folk medicine for catarrh, weak sight, pimples, rheumatism, chilblains and alcoholism! They contain oils useful in the manufacture of soaps, candles and vanishing creams, and as they also stimulate the growth of hair, in hair lotions.

Fresh bell peppers have an extremely high vitamin C content, as well as vitamins A and E. They contain 15 calories per 100 g, are 93% water and contain a few mineral salts. They are imported from Spain, Holland, Cyprus, Egypt, Italy and Kenya.

At their best fresh and crisp in salads, bell peppers are also good with dips and cheese dishes, and make a delicate sauce. They are often added to kebabs, and can be pickled or made into jellies. They feature in ratatouille, chilli con carne and pizzas, and are delicious as a stuffed vegetable. Pipérade is a famous Basque egg dish with peppers, and Peporanata gets its name from its principal ingredient.

PIPÉRADE

Pipérade is highly nostalgic food. Its strong, rustic tastes conjuring up memories of Provençal landscapes and Mediterranean sun, recalling simple yet memorable meals *al fresco*. This dish, so easy to prepare, makes a perfect meal in itself served with a tossed green salad, fresh granary bread and a bottle of the local red wine.

Per person:
1 tablespoon olive oil
1 oz (25 g) ham, cut into strips
¼ green pepper, chopped
2 tomatoes, skinned
2 eggs, beaten
salt and pepper

Heat the olive oil gently and cook the ham, peppers and tomatoes in it until they are soft and well amalgamated. Turn the heat up a little, then stir the eggs into the pan until they begin to scramble lightly, then transfer on to a warm plate and serve immediately.

CARDOON
Cynara cardunculus

The cardoon, like its relative the globe artichoke, is an edible thistle, a native of the Mediterranean coastline and now cultivated for its leaf stalks. Dioscorides mentions it as being grown on a large scale near Carthage, and Pliny extols its medicinal qualities. It got its name from a 16th century French word *carde* meaning 'prickly flowerhead', and the modern Italian word for thistle is *cardo*.

These flowerheads can be eaten when very young, before they open, and the leaves can be treated like spinach. But cardoon is grown principally for the tender white inner leaf stalks which are blanched up in the earth like celery. Choose crisp, young ones, avoiding hard or wilted stems, and cut them into 3 inch (7.5 cm) lengths. In Piedmont these are traditionally served raw, to dip into *bagna cauda*, a disastrously delicious mixture of oil, butter, anchovies and garlic. Alternatively you can steam or boil them until tender. After 10–15 minutes remove any stringy bits and then continue cooking for a further 25 minutes. Serve in a sauce *fines herbes*, or cook them in a cream sauce with a thick coating of grated parmesan cheese. Cardoon makes a delicate soup and is also delicious in salads, in a stir-fry of vegetables, à la Grecque, or deep-fried in batter.

The down of cardoon flowers is used as a substitute for rennet in the manufacture of cheese, and the plant yields a yellow dye.

CARDOON À LA GRECQUE

This classic treatment, with its characteristic coriander flavour, brings out the best in cardoon. Sliced,
and served cold in its aromatic liquid, cardoon *à la
Grecque* makes an interesting starter or buffet table
dish.

¾ pint (450 ml) water
4 tablespoons olive oil
4 tablespoons lemon juice
½ teaspoon salt
a bouquet garni of herbs
12 peppercorns
6 coriander seeds
1 lb (450 g) cardoon stalks, washed and sliced thinly

Mix the water, oil, lemon juice, salt, bouquet garni
and spices in a saucepan and simmer together for
10–15 minutes. Add the sliced cardoon and cook for
a further 10–12 minutes until it is tender. Lift out
the cardoon slices with a slotted spoon and boil the
liquid down until well-reduced, to about ⅓ pint
(200 ml). Remove the bouquet garni.

   Arrange the cardoon slices in a shallow dish, pour
the liquid over the top and leave to cool. Serve
chilled.

For 4

CELERIAC

Apium graveolens, var. *rapceum*

Celeriac was developed from celery, which gave it its name in the 18th century. It is also called 'Turnip-rooted celery' 'Celery Rave' and 'Knob Celery' as well as – inaccurately – 'Celery-root'. Its generic name *apium* comes from the Latin for a bee, since the plant attracts bees with its fragrance. *Graveolens* means strong-smelling.

The garden-designer and seedsman Stephen Switzer introduced celeriac into Britain from southern Europe in the 1720s. He had obtained seed from Alexandria and was the first to use the name celeriac in print, in a pamphlet on 'Growing Foreign Kitchen Vegetables'.

In folk medicine, oil extracted from all members

of the celery family was said to restore sexual potency after illness, and was also used to calm hysterical and nervous patients. The oil, apiol, was also applied to rheumatism and to skin diseases, and a decoction was found to be a diuretic and stimulant.

Celeriac is now exported from Holland, Israel, northern Europe and the UK. It looks like a rough brown turnip, although it is not in fact a root but the swollen stem-base of a type of celery. In size it is anything between an apple and a coconut, but since large ones may be woody and hollow, it is best to select the smaller ones. Look for firm roots, a smooth light brown and cream coloured surface, and no signs of rotting on the skin. Celeriac will keep for up to five days in the salad drawer. It is a good source of potassium and vitamin C, and contains 14 calories per 100 g.

Celeriac discolours easily when cut, so put it into acidulated water whilst peeling and cutting up. Cook it in boiling water for 15–20 minutes according to size, with a slice of lemon added to the water to keep the flesh white. Alternatively you can cut it into strips and steam. It is delicious in sauces, and makes an excellent purée either on its own or mixed with potato. Its rich celery flavour and texture are lovely raw, and traditionally julienned into Celeriac Remoulade, or mixed with Dijon mustard and thick yoghurt. Thin slivers of celeriac, stir-fried, add crunch and taste to mixed vegetables, and they can also be deep-fried like chips. Celeriac soup is warming and full of flavour, and the boiled vegetable makes a delicious *gratin* with tomatoes.

CELERIAC REMOULADE

This starter was invented by the French and is a marvellous winter food.

2 medium celeriac roots
1–2 tablespoons curry paste
1/4 pint (150 ml) mayonnaise
a little cream (optional)

Peel the celeriac carefully, then slice it thinly and cut into julienne strips. Mix the curry paste into the mayonnaise and add a little cream to thin it out if you like. Mix in the celeriac and toss thoroughly until well-coated all over. Allow to stand for an hour or so before serving. Enough for six.

CELERIAC AND POTATO PURÉE

A delectable version of mashed potato, which is delicious with roast birds or grilled fish.

1 medium celeriac root, peeled
12 oz (350 g) potatoes, peeled
1 oz (25 g) butter
4–5 tablespoons milk
salt and pepper

Boil the celeriac with the potatoes until they are tender, about 15–18 minutes. Drain, then mash with butter and milk to a smooth purée. Season to taste, and serve hot. Enough for four.

CHAYOTE
Sechium edule

Also called 'Christophine', 'Custard Marrow', 'Vegetable Pear' and 'Chow-chow', the chayote is a variety of squash and native of Mexico. It is now cultivated all over the world in tropical zones. It was well-known to the Aztecs and Mayas as a valuable food plant, for the young shoots and leaves are edible, as is the large tuberous root which can weigh up to 20 lb (9 kg).

The chayote 'fruit' is the size and shape of a large pear, growing to up to 8 inches (20 cm) long and weighing from 6–12 oz (170–340 g). There are three main varieties on the market: a light green one, a creamy white and a large, spiny dark green variety. All contain a single edible seed. The flesh should be firm, white and crisp, its delicate flavour lying somewhere between that of a cucumber and a courgette. It is excellent treated in the same way as the latter.

Peeled and de-seeded, the flesh can be sliced or diced, lightly steamed and served in a cheese sauce, or it is excellent deep-fried in batter. Chayote soup is a light, subtle starter. This vegetable is delicious either baked or boiled and then stuffed, or served simply with a peppery sauce. It goes well in curries and gives a crunch to chutneys. A good salad vegetable too, blanched or raw, chayote has a high water content and only 29 calories per 100 g.

CHAYOTE SOUP

The very gentle flavour of chayote makes a wonderful chilled soup, the palest of delicate greens. The sprinkling of dill over the top is an elegant touch, and the two flavours go beautifully together.

2 medium chayotes, peeled and cored
½ pint (300 ml) water
1 Spanish onion, peeled and sliced
salt and pepper
1 oz (25 g) butter or margarine
1 tablespoon flour
½ pint (300 ml) stock
1 bay leaf
¼ pint (150 ml) single cream
a little grated lemon rind
1 tablespoon fresh dill, chopped finely

Chop the peeled chayotes and simmer in the water with the onion, salt and pepper for about 12–15 minutes until very soft. Liquidise to a thin purée.

Melt the butter and stir in the flour, then gradually add the stock, stirring so that it becomes smooth. Add the bay leaf and allow to simmer very gently for 5 minutes. Then gradually add the chayote purée and simmer over a low heat for a few more minutes, stirring. Finally stir in the cream and grated lemon rind. Check the seasoning, remove the bay leaf, and chill.

Serve sprinkled with fresh, chopped dill.

For 4

CHICORY
Cichorium intybus

According to the oldest translation of the Bible, chicory was one of the 'bitter herbs' which God commanded the Israelites to eat with lamb at the feast of the Passover. The Greeks and Romans knew and appreciated it, and it eventually travelled to England in the 16th century. By the second half of the 18th century the roasted root of chicory began to be used to flavour coffee, to give it a bitter taste and dark colour, but soon this practice was abused and used to adulterate it. This led to a ban on the use of chicory in coffee in 1832, although by 1840 a new law permitted its inclusion so long as the coffee was correctly labelled.

Chicory is called endive in the US, and in Belgium it is known as *witloof* or 'white leaf'. Local names include 'Goat's Beard' and 'Blue Succory'. Its generic name comes from the Greek for a country road, since that was its main habitat. The lovely blue flowers, known to country folk as 'watchers of the road', were used by them as time-keepers, opening as they do in the early morning and closing at around 4 pm. The leaves yield a blue dye, and in Germany and Italy chicory seed used to be sold as a panacea, and particularly as a love-philtre. Other uses in folk medicine included the treatment of jaundice, liver enlargement, gout and skin eruptions. It was used as a tonic, for its laxative and diuretic properties.

Chicory is a native of western Asia and is nowadays cultivated by blanching up the leaves under layers of sand or peat, to prevent the formation of chlorophyll pigments – green chicory leaves are extremely bitter. When so grown it is conical in shape, about 4–6 inches (10–15 cm) long, with a slightly sharp flavour, and should be white and crisp. Choose even-sized tight heads, avoiding aging ones with green tips, and keep well wrapped in the salad drawer for up to three days. Chicory is at its best from September to February, although it is now available from around the world for most of the year.

Chicory makes a crisp and refreshing salad vegetable, especially good when mixed with oranges and nuts. It contains 9 calories per 100 g, tiny amounts of vitamins B and C, and a little potassium. It is also delicious braised with butter and served as a side vegetable. Cooked, it can be mixed into a cream sauce or served with *beurre noisette*, or sliced and deep-fried in batter. It is delicious *à la Grecque*, or made into a purée, or used to make a soufflé.

CHICORY AND HAM GRATINÉE

Cooked chicory becomes very delicate in flavour; it has a unique texture and makes a marvellous marriage with ham and a creamy cheese sauce.

8 heads of chicory
16 thin slices of ham
1 oz (25 g) butter or margarine
2 tablespoons flour
¼ pint (150 ml) milk, warmed
3 oz (75 g) Gruyère, grated
5 tablespoons single cream
1 tablespoon grated parmesan
salt and pepper

Cook the chicory in boiling water until soft, about 8 minutes. Drain thoroughly and cool. Then wrap each one up in a slice of ham and place in a well-greased baking dish.

Melt the butter or margarine in a small, heavy pan and stir in the flour. Stir until it is heated through, then gradually add the warmed milk, stirring all the time until the sauce is smooth and thick. Allow to bubble very gently for 5 minutes, then stir in the grated Gruyère and the cream and season to taste with salt and pepper. Pour this over the chicory and ham, and sprinkle with the parmesan.

Bake in a preheated oven at 350°F/180°C/Gas 4 for 15 minutes until browned on top.

For 4

EDDOE
Colocasia esculenta, var. *antiquorum*

First recorded by the Chinese nearly 2,000 years ago, the eddoe is a variety of taro, a kind of tuber, and is a native of south east Asia. It travelled from India to Egypt and was introduced into Europe when the Arabs brought it to Spain during our Dark Ages. They say that Captain Cook was probably the first Englishman to breakfast on it! It is also called 'Chinese Potato', 'Egyptian Ginger' and 'Taro'.

Eddoes are brown, hairy tubers consisting of a central corm around which grow smaller cormels, either round or elongated and weighing from 1 ounce to 1 lb (25–450 g). They should be full and sound, firm to the touch. The flesh is usually snowy-white, although there are yellow, pink and orange varieties.

The flavour is not dissimilar to a potato, but pleasantly nuttier, and the eddoe should be stored in the same way as the potato. It is very digestible, containing a fine-grained starch rather like arrowroot. Its slight stickiness when peeled can be reduced by soaking in acidulated water for half an hour. You can roast eddoes like potatoes around a joint of meat, mash them with butter and a little milk, or slice them finely and deep-fry them like chips. They are delicious in a pork or chicken casserole and excellent in curries. There is a traditional West African recipe called 'Fufu', in which eddoes are made into dumplings to serve with spicy stews and soups.

CHICKEN AND EDDOE CURRY

A substantial and warming dish. The spiciness of the garlic and garam masala are a perfect complement to the bland eddoe.

1½ pints (900 ml) boiling water
2 oz (50 g) desiccated coconut
2 tablespoons vegetable oil
2 cloves of garlic, crushed
2 tablespoons garam masala
1 3-lb (1.5-kg) chicken, skinned and cut into small joints
the juice of half a lemon
a 2 inch (5 cm) piece of lemon rind
2 small onions, sliced
6 medium eddoes, peeled and diced
salt to taste

To make the coconut milk, pour the boiling water over the desiccated coconut and leave to stand for 30 minutes. Stir, then strain off.

Heat the oil and fry the garlic and garam masala gently until well amalgamated. Then stir in the chicken pieces with the lemon juice and rind and half of the coconut milk. Bring to the boil, then lower the heat and add the rest of the coconut milk, the onion and the eddoes. Simmer until both the chicken and the eddoes are cooked, about 25 minutes. Check the seasoning and discard the lemon rind. Add the lemon juice, stir well and serve hot with basmati rice or naan.

For 4–6

FENNEL
Foeniculum vulgare

Florence fennel is the swollen stem-base of the fennel plant, composed of tightly compressed swathes of fleshy leaves rather similar in structure to an onion. It is a native of Italy and has a long history. Fennel was enjoyed not only by the Greeks and Romans but by the ancient Egyptians also. It was introduced into England around 1750, and was cultivated mainly in and around Hitchin in Hertfordshire – indeed one of its common names used to be simply 'Hitchin'. It travelled to America at the end of the 18th century and the statesman Thomas Jefferson grew it in his garden at Monticello. He was sent two varieties of Italian seed in 1824 by Thomas Appleton, one of his American consuls, and is quoted as saying 'The fennel is, beyond every other vegetable, delicious. There is no vegetable to equal it in flavour. I preferred it to every other vegetable; or to any fruit.'

In folk medicine fennel has been found to be a good digestive; it has a soothing action on the stomach, with a carminative effect. An infusion of fennel seed used to be prescribed for insomnia, and a decoction of fennel as a gargle. A less likely cure is to pound the roots of fennel with honey as a remedy for the bite of a mad dog.

Fennel's name derives from the Greek *foeniculum*, meaning 'little hay', because of its feathery, finely-cut leaves with their sweet smell.

There are many varieties of fennel, and supplies now come from Spain and Holland as well as Italy. Fennel measures about 4–5 inches (10–13 cm) across, and can weigh up to 1 lb (450 g). It has a licorice flavour and an aromatic, aniseed taste. Choose well-rounded ones, unblemished and white or very pale green. Trim the base and the top, reserving the leaves for adding flavour to the dish, or for garnish. Fennel will store in the fridge for up to five days, and although available all the year round it is more plentiful during the summer months.

Sliced into salads, fennel gives crunch as well as distinctive flavour. It is also delicious steamed or boiled and served in a cheese sauce. It makes a perfect partner to fish, and can be sliced and deep-fried in batter and served with a Pernod-flavoured mayonnaise. Fennel soup is sublime, the vegetable makes a delicate soufflé, and it is wonderful with pasta. It also goes very well with a cheeseboard.

FENNEL FRITTERS

These fritters are epicurean!

2 heads of fennel

For the batter:
4 oz (100 g) plain flour
a pinch of salt
3 tablespoons vegetable oil
¼ pint (150 ml) warm water
1 egg white

Sift the flour with the salt and stir in the oil. Gradually add the water, stirring until thick and creamy. Leave to stand in a cool place for 2 hours, then add a little more water to thin it out. It should be the consistency of thin cream. Beat the egg white until very stiff, and fold into the batter just before you use it.

Simmer or steam the fennel heads until tender, about 15 minutes. Allow them to cool, then cut each one in half and cut into ¼ inch (5 mm) slices. Dip into the batter and deep-fry in very hot oil until puffed and golden all over. Drain on kitchen paper, sprinkle with a little salt, and serve as soon as possible.

For 4

FENNEL AND WALNUT SALAD

A party piece! The slightly aniseed flavour of fennel goes beautifully with the strong taste of walnuts, both nuts and oil.

2 small heads of fennel, sliced
3 oz (75 g) walnuts, chopped
4 tablespoons walnut oil
a squeeze of lemon juice

Combine all the ingredients and marinate for 1 hour before serving.

For 4

GLOBE ARTICHOKE

Cynara solymus

The globe artichoke, a member of the thistle family, is a native of the Mediterranean coast of North Africa and is now exported from Brittany, Provence, Italy and Spain. Artichokes have been in cultivation for thousands of years, ever since the ancient Egyptians grew them. 'Food for the gods' to the Romans, the reputation of the artichoke as an aphrodisiac later became so scandalous that no decent woman would be seen eating one!

They were introduced into Britain in about 1548 as 'archecokks', and Henry VIII is reputed to have liked them because they were both a tonic for the liver and an aphrodisiac. These thistles, decorative and gastronomic plants in one, became the aristocrats of the Renaissance kitchen garden, a fashion set by Queen Henrietta Maria (1609–69) who had an artichoke garden at her manor at Wimbledon. Catherine de Medici, who was responsible for bringing artichokes to the tables of France from Florence in the 16th century, ate so many at a wedding feast in 1575 that – so the story goes – she nearly burst!

By the 19th century, however, the popularity of John Evelyn's 'noble thistle' was at its nadir; said one cookery writer, 'It is good for a man to eat thistles, and to remember that he is an ass.'

Artichokes are mid to dark green in colour with a purplish tinge, about 5 inches (13 cm) in diameter,

and should be plump and round in shape and heavy for their size. The 'heart' of the artichoke, which is actually the base of the flower, is sweet and meaty, as are the bases of each leaf scale and top of the stem. Although available from May to September, they are at their best in July and August. They will keep in the fridge for up to three days, but once cooked should be eaten on the same day. They have a high water content and contain 15 calories per 100 g, 2% carbohydrate, and vitamins A and C.

To prepare an artichoke, cut the tips off the leafy scales and trim the stem to about ½ inch (1.5 cm). Soak in cold water to release any grit or insects, then boil or steam for about 40 minutes. For stuffed artichokes, drain and cool them, then remove the hairy 'choke' and discard it. Fill the cavity with creamed shellfish, vegetable purées or hollandaise sauce. Very young and tender artichokes are eaten raw in Italy and Spain, and whole baby ones are deep-fried in batter, as are the hearts, or stewed in oil. Artichokes can be eaten either hot or cold, dipping the succulent parts into melted butter, vinaigrette or mayonnaise, and a whole variety of sauces.

Artichauts Farcis Provençales

The pungent flavours of olives, herbs and garlic, so characteristic of Mediterranean cookery, make a delicious filling for cold artichokes.

4 globe artichokes
6 tablespoons chopped parsley
2 cloves of garlic, crushed
8 black olives, stoned and chopped
1 tablespoon dried mixed herbs
2 tablespoons grated parmesan
salt and pepper
½ pint (300 ml) mayonnaise

Soak the artichokes in cold water for about half an hour to remove any grit or insects. Trim the stalks, and cut the tips off all the leaves. Cook in boiling, salted water for 40 minutes or until tender. Drain and cool, then remove the central leaves. Lift the hairy choke off the heart with the blade of a knife, scraping the surface clear.

Combine the parsley, garlic, olives and herbs with the parmesan and season to taste. Mix into the mayonnaise and pile a quarter of the mixture into each artichoke. Serve with warm garlic bread.

For 4

KOHL RABI
Brassica caulorapa or
oleracea, var. *gongyloides*

Kohl rabi was first taken from Italy to Germany in the mid 16th century, and it has been cultivated in France for several hundred years, where it is known as *choux raves*. However, it has only been grown in England since the early 19th century – and then originally for cattle fodder, although Mrs Beeton in 1861 charitably called it 'wholesome, nutritious and very palatable.' Kohl rabi has been used in Chinese medicine for many centuries, and is grown in the Far East for that reason. It was found to cure a wide variety of minor ailments, to prevent sickness and to keep the body in balance.

Kohl rabi is in fact the swollen stem-base of a member of the cabbage family, with a delicate turnip-like flavour which has given it the name of 'Turnip-rooted Cabbage' and 'Stem Turnip'. It contains a large amount of vitamin C and some mineral salts, and has 23 calories to every 100 g. Available during the winter months, it can be kept in the salad drawer for 2–3 days.

Choose kohl rabi which are no larger than a tennis ball, because larger ones tend to be tough in texture and strong in taste. Make sure that they are not wizened or pitted with worm holes, and just cut off the stalk, scrub and slice it. For the best flavour, steam until tender but still slightly crisp, about 10 minutes, and serve in a cheesy sauce, or tossed in melted butter with basil. Raw, it can be grated into salads or mixed with a lightly curried mayonnaise. It adds distinction to a macedoine of vegetables, and makes excellent fritters.

LAMBS' LETTUCE
Valerianella locusta

Indigenous from the west coast of Ireland to the Caucasus, lamb's lettuce is so-called either because sheep show a predilection for it or because its leaves are at their greenest at the end of winter when lambing starts. It is good winter salading, growing like a weed on waste ground and around cornfields, giving it its other names 'Corn Salad' and 'Field Lettuce'. Known to the French as *Mâche*, it is also called *Salade de Prêtre* because it was eaten during Lenten fasts, and 'Loblollie' because – according to Gerard – it was an ingredient of a sailors' gruel of the same name. It was also used as a spring tonic by country folk, being one of the few fresh greens around after a long winter's diet of salted meat.

Lambs' lettuce grows from 6–12 inches (15–30 cm) tall and the leaves measure about 2 inches (5 cm) across. They are tongue-shaped and bright green, hence another name of 'Lamb's Tongue'. It was introduced into Britain from the Netherlands about 400 years ago, and although commercially grown in Italy it is mostly exported to the UK from France. When fresh, it has a soft texture and nutty, slightly astringent flavour which is delicious simply dressed with walnut oil, or mixed with thinly sliced beetroot in a vinaigrette.

It makes a lovely 'hot and cold' salad: a mixture of different salad leaves, bacon and crisp croûtons of fried bread, over which is poured a hot dressing, which is made by sizzling little cubes of streaky bacon in a frying pan until the fat runs. You then pour in a tablespoon of vinegar and let it sizzle and reduce for a few moments. Pour in enough olive oil for the dressing, heat it through and pour it over the assembled salad.

Lamb's Lettuce can also be cooked like spinach, and should be stored in much the same way, in a plastic bag in a salad drawer, where it will keep for 2–3 days.

LOTUS ROOT
Nelumbium nuciferum

The languor-inducing fruit eaten by the Lotus Eaters in Homer's *Odyssey*, this 'Water-lily of the Nile' was grown in ancient Egypt and is even depicted in their sculpture. The Hindu lotus, or Sacred Lotus, is a native of Asia and has been cultivated since antiquity for its beauty. It is still a holy and mystical plant in India, China and Japan, the growth of the flower through water and air to rise above the water representing the soul's search for nirvana.

The root looks like plump sugar cane, or – less poetically – a string of sausages. Inside its thin, buff-coloured, tough skin the flesh is white and crisp, and patterned with holes like a mincer blade. Young, it can be eaten raw in salads, whereas older specimens are cooked like potatoes until tender. They taste a little like artichoke hearts with an edge to them. They range from 5–12 inches (13–30 cm) in length and from 2–3 inches (5–7 cm) in diameter. Unblemished roots keep for up to three weeks in the salad drawer. Lotus roots are also available dried in some Chinese supermarkets.

Lotus roots are often served as part of a tempura platter, and big roots are steamed and stuffed. They can be fried, or lightly boiled and served like asparagus. They simply need peeling and dropping into acidulated water before cooking, in order to prevent discoloration.

MANGE-TOUT PEAS
Pisum sativum, var. *saccaratum*

'Eat them all peas' is a good description of this thin-podded variety of pea, of which the entire fruit is eaten. It has been grown in England for the past 150 years and is considered by many to be in the asparagus class. Its flavour is distinctive and slightly sweet, its texture crunchy yet tender, and mange-touts lend themselves to cooking in a variety of ways. Lightly steamed and tossed in a little butter, they make one of the very best side vegetables to go with tender spring lamb or with grilled fish. Cooled, they make an original salad with slivered browned almonds. They make a superlative soup, and can be thinly sliced diagonally and tossed into a Chinese stir-fry of vegetables. Raw, they are sweet and crunchy in a summer salad.

Choose bright green, firm, fresh mange-touts which are juicy but whose peas do not protrude too much. Store in a plastic bag to preserve their quality, and keep in the salad drawer for up to 3 days. To prepare them, top and tail, snapping off the stalk and pulling backwards to remove the coarse thread along the side.

Mange-touts contain 67 calories per 100 g, and vitamins A and C. They are also known as 'Chinese Peas' and 'Snow Peas'. Although available home grown in the early summer, they are now imported from Kenya and the US in winter, and from Jersey, France and Spain throughout the summer months.

MOOLI
Raphanus sativus, var. *longipinnatus*

Mooli is a giant radish that can grow up to 12 inches (30 cm) long and 3 inches (7.5 cm) in diameter, or even larger in some Japanese varieties. It is also known as 'Rettich', 'Daikon', 'Icicle Radish' and 'Chinese', 'Japanese', 'Oriental' or 'White' radish. It has been used since ancient times as food, and the Chinese also valued it for its digestive and diuretic properties. It is recorded that the labourers working on the Great Pyramids ate radishes and garlic, and so respected was it by the ancient Greeks that they laid radishes of gold outside Apollo's temple at Delphi.

Mooli should look clear and bright and be hard to the touch. The skin is thin and white with a few rootlets, and its flavour is milder than that of the slightly hot red radish.

Peel it, slice it thinly or grate it and add to salads. Or shred it into soups for texture, or cut it into julienne strips and lightly steam it for a gentler flavour. The Japanese soak strips of it in water for 30 minutes or so before serving it with raw fish; they also use it, cut into decorative shapes, as a garnish. In the East it is frequently curried and pickled, and is delicious grated into yoghurt as a raita to go with spicy foods. Try serving slices of mooli with a cheeseboard instead of celery – it goes particularly well with cream cheese and goat cheeses – or presenting it as a nibble to go with drinks before a meal, to cleanse the palate.

Mooli contains 19–24 calories per 100 g, various mineral salts and small amounts of vitamins A and C.

MOOLI PICKLE

This unusual dry pickle is based on a Malaysian recipe. Serve it with a curry or to spice up salads which have blander flavours. It keeps for up to six weeks in the fridge.

1 tablespoon vegetable oil
1 tablespoon mustard seeds
2 teaspoons turmeric powder
3 teaspoons salt
2 large mooli, grated coarsely
4 fresh chillies, seeded and cut in half lengthwise
10 small shallots, peeled and cut in half
1/2 pint (300 ml) white wine vinegar
5 oz (150 g) salted peanuts, ground coarsely

Heat the oil in a large pan and fry the mustard seeds in it until they pop. Turn the heat down and add the turmeric and salt. Stir for a minute or two, then add the mooli, chillies and shallots. Fry for about 5 minutes, then pour in the vinegar and bring to the boil. Finally stir in the coarsely ground peanuts, heat through again and then remove from the heat. Cool completely, then store in airtight jars.

OKRA
Hibiscus esculentus

Thisannual member of the exotic cotton family –
a hibiscus, no less – has slender, hexagonal
green pods about 3–5 inches (7.5–13 cm) in length
with tender green skins that mark easily. These
immature seed pods, with their slightly fuzzy skins,
occur frequently in African, Indian and Middle
Eastern recipes and get their name from an 18th
century Gold Coast word 'nkurama'. Known in
Egypt by the 13th century, okra travelled to America with the slave trade and were first recorded there
in the mid 18th century. Their elegant shape gave
them the name 'Ladies' Fingers' and they are also
known as 'Gumbo' because they become sticky and
gummy when over cooked.

Okra have found their way into Indian folk medicine, where they were used to treat disorders of the

genito-urinary tract. They were also found to be of use in chest infections because of their emollient quality.

Now exported from the Caribbean and Kenya, Central America and Cyprus, okra contains 17 calories per 100 g, 90% water, 7% carbohydrate, some mineral salts and vitamins A and C. The only preparation needed is to rinse, top and tail them, and then steam or simmer for 4–6 minutes before tossing in a little butter to serve as a side vegetable. Choose young okra, since older ones tend to be stringy, and select bright firm ones with no traces of brown on them. You can soak them in water with a little added vinegar for an hour before cooking to remove the glueyness.

Okra turns slightly mucilaginous on cooking and adds an almost jelly-like smoothness to sauces. They are delicious fried with chicken, and are especially good with tomatoes and seafood. They go well with rice and often feature in Indian curries as *bhindi*. Their flavour and texture are as good hot as cold, they are superb deep-fried in light batter, and are an indispensible ingredient in Middle Eastern Bamia, in Creole Gumbo and in West Indian Callaloo.

BAMIA

Bamia is a classic Middle Eastern dish, usually served cold so that all the delicious flavours can permeate each other. The taste of coriander with the soft, fleshy okra is scrumptious. Serve it as a starter with warm pitta bread.

1½ lb (675 g) okra
4–5 tablespoons olive oil
10 small shallots, peeled and sliced
1 medium bunch fresh coriander
6 cloves of garlic, crushed
3 tomatoes, sliced
lemon juice
salt

Wash and dry the okra well, and cut off the tops. Fry in olive oil until tender but still firm. Remove from the pan and fry the shallots until they are softened. Blend the coriander leaves and the garlic together in the food processor and add this purée to the softened shallots in the pan. Stir-fry for a few minutes.

Put the sliced tomatoes in the bottom of a heatproof casserole. Arrange the okra neatly on top, and cover with the shallot and coriander mixture. Sprinkle with lemon juice and add a few drops of water. Cover the dish with foil and then with a closely-fitting lid, and place over a low heat for 25–30 minutes. Remove the lid and the foil, stir the mixture and check the seasoning. Cool and chill.

For 4

PAK CHOI AND PE-TSAI
Brassica chinensis and *Brassica pekinensis*

Chinese cabbage, as Pe-tsai is most commonly known, is grown mostly for its use as a winter and autumn vegetable. Other names include 'Tientsin Cabbage' and 'Celery Cabbage.' It looks rather like a pale cos lettuce with soft green and white veined leaves which have wavy margins. It is crisp and crunchy when raw, with a flavour between lettuce and cabbage. It is an excellent vehicle for other flavours, and the small inner leaves are delicious raw, eaten like asparagus with hollandaise sauce. Pe-tsai, which means 'white vegetable', retains its delicacy and crunchiness in stir-frying. The inner leaves, grated and gratinéed, make an original hors d'oeuvre. Store in a plastic bag in the fridge.

Pak choi is also a variety of cabbage, but more closely related to rape and swede than to our everyday cabbage, and looks rather like chard or spinach-beet. It has broad, smooth-edged leaves which taper into a narrow-margined stalk between 10 and 20 inches (25–50 cm) long. It is also known as 'Chinese Mustard' and 'Mustard Greens', and when cooked has a flavour not unlike that of broccoli. Leaves and stalks, shredded and cooked together like spinach, are a bright green and delicious simply tossed in a little butter, or creamed in a white sauce, used as a stuffing for pancakes or stir-fried and added to rice. Very finely shredded and deep-fried, pak choi is the 'seaweed' often served in Chinese restaurants.

Both varieties originated in Asia and eastern China and have been eaten since the 5th century BC. They were introduced into Europe at the end of the 18th century and are now available all year round, imported from Israel, Holland and Spain.

STIR-FRY CHINESE LEAVES

Stir-frying brings out the best in crisp Chinese leaves. They are cooked just long enough to heat through, yet retain their appetising texture. In this dish their subtle flavour is highlighted with ginger, garlic and soy sauce. A quick, easy and delicious side vegetable.

3 tablespoons sesame oil
1 inch (2.5 cm) root ginger, grated
2 cloves of garlic, crushed
4 oz (100 g) small button mushrooms, halved
12 oz (350 g) Chinese leaves, shredded
4–5 tablespoons soy sauce

Heat the oil in a large pan or wok and stir-fry the grated ginger and garlic for 2 minutes. Add the mushrooms and stir-fry for a further minute or two, then add the Chinese leaves and toss until well-coated in the oil. Heat through, stirring all the time, then add the soy sauce and cook for another minute. Serve immediately.

For 4

PLANTAIN
Musa paradisiaca

The plantain is a 'cooking banana', originally grown in India and southern Asia over 3,000 years ago. Larger than its yellow cousin, which is so commonly eaten as fruit throughout the world, and with a higher starch and lower sugar content, the plantain is used when green and unripe and is a chief staple food for millions of people in East Africa.

Also known as *Figuier d'Adam*, according to Hindu legend the banana was the forbidden fruit of the Paradise garden – which they believed was situated in Ceylon. It was with the leaves from this tree that man covered his nakedness. In other parts of the world they are known as 'Macho Bananas'!

Plantains have dry, starchy, fibrous flesh with 112 calories per 100 g and vitamins A and C. They can be sliced and fried as chips, and in India are often curried with the skins left on. They can be cooked whole in their skins, roasted or barbecued, or boiled for about 30 minutes until tender. Fried plantain goes well with fish and meat dishes, and the flesh can also be used in sweet dishes. They should be stored at room temperature, not refrigerated, and can be cooked either skinned and chopped or left whole.

Plantains have had their uses in folk medicine as a laxative, to relieve diarrhoea, to treat respiratory problems and as a dressing for skin lesions. The Indians maintain that ripe plantain and ghee restores virility.

PLANTAIN TOSTONES

A Caribbean wayside snack, these scrumptious morsels make an unusual nibble to go with drinks, and are also a delicious accompaniment to roasted meat.

1 large plantain, peeled
salted water
vegetable oil for frying
salt

Cut the plantain into diagonal slices about ¼ inch (5 mm) thick, and soak in salted water for 30 minutes. Drain and dry thoroughly, then sauté in oil until they are tender but not crisp on the outside. Drain on kitchen paper.

Put the plantain slices between sheets of greaseproof paper. Flatten them down evenly with a rolling pin until they are half their original thickness. Then sauté them again until they are golden-brown and crisp all over. Drain once more on kitchen paper, sprinkle with salt, and serve as soon as possible.

Makes 20

SALSIFY AND SCORZONERA
Tragopagon porrifolius and *scorzonera hispanica*

Both salsify and scorzonera are natives of southern Europe, and are long carrot-shaped roots with a succulence and delicacy that have given them the reputation of being a luxury vegetable, with local names of 'Vegetable Oyster' and 'Oyster Plant'. Scorzonera is known as 'Black Salsify' because of its black skin, whereas salsify has a whitish, parsnip-like skin and is also known as 'Purple Goat's Beard' because of its wispy purple flowers. The name salsify itself comes from 'solsequium', the flower that follows the course of the sun, and it has a quaint

local name of 'Nap at Noon'. Scorzonera, also 'Serpent's Root' and 'Viper's Grass', comes from the Catalan *escorso*, or viper, as it was thought to be a remedy for their venom. It also means 'black bark' in Spanish.

Both were originally developed in Italy and became very popular in Spain and Germany around the 13th century. They arrived in England and France in the late 17th century, and are now imported from Holland and Belgium. They are usually available from autumn to late spring.

Scorzonera was first cultivated as a medicinal plant, used as an aperient and anti-bilious herb. Gerard describes its uses to treat 'obstructions of gall' and in cases of jaundice. It contains insulin, a sugar that can be eaten by diabetics.

Choose firm, plump roots and handle them carefully, scraping off the skin rather than peeling as they tend to 'bleed'. They contain 18 calories per 100 g, vegetable protein, mineral salts and vitamin C. Store the fresh roots in a cold dark place for up to two days. Top and tail them, cut them into 3-inch (7.5 cm) lengths and drop into acidulated water whilst peeling them.

Steam or boil salsify and scorzonera until tender, about 15 minutes. Both make a delicious soup, and are very good as a salad vegetable, either pre-cooked or grated raw into mayonnaise. They are excellent gratinéed or served in sauces, and chunks of salsify are a delicate addition to a chicken pie, served either hot or cold. The roots make an asparagus-like hors d'oeuvre when served with *beurre noisette*.

SQUASHES
Cucurbitaceae spp.

Squashes or gourds are one of the oldest vegetables known to man – indeed many have Sanskrit names which reveal their antiquity. Remains of squash have been found in Mexican caves dating back to 7000 BC, and in Egyptian tombs of 3500 BC. The Romans used them, and they were cultivated by American Indians long before the arrival of Columbus. First grown in Britain in the 16th century for food, by the time of the Victorian era they were being grown competitively for their size and for decoration, and are only now beginning to re-appear on the English table, having closer associations for many with a Hallowe'en Jack o'lantern.

There are over 750 species in the family, the most well-known being the 'Butternut Squash', 'Vegetable Spaghetti', 'Acorn Squash', 'Canada' or 'Japanese Squash', and 'summer' and 'autumn Pumpkins'. There is a 'Turban Squash' (*Bonnet de Prêtre*), a 'Golden Nugget Squash', 'Pattypan' or 'Custard Marrow', 'Crookneck Squash' and 'Ridged Gourd'. The name 'squash' derives from the 18th century and is a shortened version of the Red Indian name *askutasquash*, meaning 'fruits eaten green', or raw.

Gourds have had innumerable medicinal uses: for treating eye infections, constipation, leprosy, skin eruptions, gout, anaemia and thrush to name but some. They were believed to be a general tonic, and contain an oil that heals wounds and soothes burns and chapped skins. The sponge gourd, dried, is our 'loofah', and its fibrous interior was used for industrial filtering before the advent of modern plastics. Squashes are also known for their oily seeds, usually marketed as pumpkin seeds.

Choose firm squashes and avoid ones which are shrivelled near the stalk or have blemished skins, and don't store them for too long as they tend to go flabby. The flesh of a squash should be firm and non-fibrous, and is best eaten young. They have little nutritive value, being 94% water.

Squashes, particularly the 'Snake Gourd', are widely used in Indian curries, and they are famous in America not only in Pumpkin Pie but as a popular side-vegetable. They make delicious purées, and can be sliced and sautéed in a herb butter, or stuffed and served in the skin. The seeds are delicious deep-fried in oil and salted, and are known as *pepitos*.

STUFFED GARLIC SQUASH

Butternut squashes have the reputation of being one of the tastiest varieties, and they certainly have a delectable sweetness, a deep golden colour and an appetisingly soft texture. This herby filling is delicious with the squash flesh: the garlic, pre-cooked, loses its heat and becomes delicately aromatic, having none of the lingering after-effects of raw garlic! A delicious supper dish.

2 butternut squashes
2 heads of garlic
4 tablespoons mixed fresh herbs, chopped
1½ oz (40 g) cheddar, grated
1 egg, beaten
salt and pepper

Cut the squashes in half lengthwise and scoop out the seeds.

Separate all the cloves of garlic and simmer them in water for 6–8 minutes until soft, then cool and peel them. Put the garlic into the blender with the herbs, cheddar and beaten egg, and blend until smooth. Season to taste with salt and pepper, and pack this stuffing into the hollows of the squashes. Wrap them up separately in foil and bake in a pre-heated oven, 375°F/190°C/Gas 5, for 1 hour and 15 minutes or until tender right through. Serve with a mixed salad and warm granary rolls.

For 4

SWEET POTATO
Ipomoea batatas

The sweet potato is aptly named for its sugary taste, and it is also known as 'Louisiana Yam' and 'Long Potato'. It was cultivated in pre-historic Peru and first brought to Europe at the turn of the 16th century after the discovery of America. They flourished in Spanish soil and became widely known as Spanish potatoes. Sir Francis Drake brought some back with him from his voyages in the 1560s, and by 1577 they were easily available in London, where it became fashionable to serve them with roast beef instead of turnips or parsnips.

During the Tudor period, sweet potatoes were sold in crystallised slices rather like marrons glacés, combined with candied sea-holly. These 'kissing comfits', as Shakespeare called them, were sold as aphrodisiacs, and they began to catch on with the French when the Empress Josephine introduced them into her garden at Malmaison. Soon sweet potato comfits became the rage at intimate Parisian parties, given to lovers to stimulate their passions. John Parkinson, botanist and writer, wrote of them in 1629, 'The Spanish potatoes are roasted under the embers, and being pared or peeled and sliced, are put into sacke with a little sugar, or without, and is delicate to be eaten.' Candied sweet potatoes are still sold in France to this day, preserved in syrup.

Sweet potatoes are imported from Brazil, Israel, the West Indies, Egypt and Mexico, and are available all the year round. Native to tropical America, and not related to the ordinary potato, this starchy, swollen tuber varies in shape and size, but is usually pink to orange inside with a pinky-red skin. An average sweet potato is about 6 inches (15 cm) long, weighing 6 oz-1 lb (175–450 g). It has a sweet, chestnutty flavour and is a staple food in many poor counties. It contains 21% carbohydrate, and large amounts of vitamin A, some vitamin C, and has 91 calories per 100 g. Choose firm, unblemished specimens and keep them for up to one week in a dark, cool place.

Sweet potatoes are delicious with grilled or roast meat and poultry, and in the US are used as a pie filling. They can be baked in their skins like ordinary potatoes, or boiled, or sautéed. Cooked and sliced, they are delicious deep-fried in batter or mashed with cream and seasoned with pepper and nutmeg. Sweet potatoes, glazed or candied, are a traditional accompaniment to the Thanksgiving turkey in America. They go well in curries, make good croquettes, and a soufflé with a difference.

SWEET POTATO CROQUETTES

The unusual sweetness of this vegetable gives an original taste to croquettes when carefully spiced with pepper and nutmeg. Crispy on the outside and moist on the inside, sweet potato croquettes make a delicious side vegetable dish to go with roast meats, particularly chicken.

1 lb (450 g) sweet potatoes, peeled
2–3 tablespoons milk
½ oz (15 g) butter
salt, pepper and nutmeg
2 teaspoons grated parmesan
2 egg yolks, beaten

For frying:
seasoned flour, beaten egg and breadcrumbs
sunflower oil

Cook the sweet potatoes in boiling water until they are soft through, about 15–18 minutes. Drain them, then mash with the milk and butter so that they are smooth, but the mixture is quite stiff. Season with salt, pepper and nutmeg. Add the parmesan and finally stir in the beaten egg yolks. Chill.

Take tablespoons of the mixture and form into croquette-sized rolls. Roll them in seasoned flour, beaten egg and breadcrumbs and deep fry in hot sunflower oil until golden all over. Drain on kitchen paper and keep hot. Serve as soon as possible.

For 4

WATERCHESTNUT AND PI TSI

Trapa natans and
Eleocharis tuberosa

This member of the willowherb or sedge family has an edible seed which has been used as food since Neolithic times. It is still eaten in Central Europe and Asia, raw, roasted or boiled in much the same way as the common chestnut, for its floury texture and agreeable taste. It is part of a pretty, floating aquatic plant bearing fruit 1–2 inches (2.5–5 cm) wide with two horn-like projections which gave it its local name of 'Caltrops', an ancient war weapon with four spine-like projections. It got its name waterchestnut from its chestnut-coloured skin and watery habitat. It is also known as 'Waternuts', 'Horse's Hoof' and 'Jesuit's Bread'.

The Chinese waterchestnut, Pi Tsi, is generally thought to be more gastronomic in flavour and has a crunchier, nuttier texture rather like that of a fresh potato, and is obtained from a different variety of sedge. It is available in winter from some Chinese shops.

Both varieties are available canned but are infinitely better fresh. Choose firm, unblemished specimens with no sign of sprouting, and eat them within a week, storing them in the fridge in salted water. Keep leftover canned ones covered with fresh water in a glass jar in the fridge.

To prepare fresh waterchestnuts, wash and peel with a sharp knife before steaming them until tender but still crunchy. They are delicious sliced into stuffings, in *dim sum*, and mixed with other vegetables in spring rolls. They give a crunch to a Thai dish of pork and chillies, are a characteristic addition to a Loire Risotto, and make an unusual garnish, slivered thinly, to a dish of tiny French beans. They can be marinated and grilled, and cooked this way are an interesting addition to a vegetable stir-fry and to noodle dishes.

THAI PORK WITH WATERCHESTNUTS AND CHILLIES

This is a dish of textures – smooth cubes of fillet of pork, and crisp slices of waterchestnut, with the heat of chillies to give it zest.

1 large onion, sliced thinly
2 cloves of garlic, crushed
1 inch (2.5 cm.) root ginger, grated
4 tablespoons oil
salt
1½ lb (675 g) pork fillet, diced
1 teaspoon turmeric
4 fresh red chillies, seeded and chopped very finely
the juice of 1 lemon
¼ pint (150 ml) water
8 oz (250 g) waterchestnuts, sliced

Fry the onion, garlic and ginger in the oil until soft. Add a little salt and stir in the pork, turning so that it browns evenly all over. Stir in the turmeric and chopped chillies and mix well. Add the lemon juice and water, stir thoroughly, and continue to cook until the pork is tender. Then add the waterchestnuts and heat through for a further 5 minutes. Check the seasoning and serve with boiled rice.

For 4–6

YAM
Discorea spp.

The yam is probably a native of China but it was first discovered by westerners in Central America. It arrived in England in the 16th century, before the potato, but failed to become very popular. The yam is an important staple crop in poorer areas of the world such as Africa and Asia, and is now cultivated widely. It is also grown for animal feed, containing as it does a high starch content – 29% carbohydrate, 119 calories per 100 g, and some vitamin A and potassium.

The yam is a large, edible root of a family of plants which boasts up to 250 species. One of them, the Asiatic yam, can weigh up to 90 lb (40 kg)! It is a sweet, white or orange-fleshed tuber which stores well. The 'White Yam', most commonly on sale, weighs between 4½-11 lb (2–5 kg). It has a mealy texture which lingers even after long cooking, and its starchiness and blandness of taste need lifting with spices and sauces to make it an interesting vegetable. It has a thin bark-like skin which is rough to the feel and grey-brown in colour. The raw flesh is white and slightly sticky.

Yam can be boiled or mashed, roasted or fried in the same ways as the potato. It is a good vehicle for a curry, and excellent in mixed vegetable soups and stews. The Chinese mash yam with lotus root, wrap it in lotus leaves and then steam it. Yam fritters with sweet and sour sauce are quite a delicacy, and the vegetable can be used both in sweet and in savoury pies, having a special affinity with cinnamon. It provides a starch extract similar to arrowroot, which is widely used in cookery and confectionery.

Yams have featured quite prominently in folk medicine throughout the world. The dried rhizome has proved to be the best relief and promptest cure for bilious colic, and is an excellent remedy for morning sickness in pregnant women. It was prescribed in cases of cholera to relieve cramps, and was used as an expectorant and diuretic. Its common names of 'Colic Root' and 'Rheumatism Root' reveal its medicinal uses, and the Indians believed that it helped cure arthritis. Yam is an important source of diosgenin, used in oral contraceptives. Some species of yam are toxic when raw, and were used by natives on poisonous hunting weapons – so it is unwise to eat yam uncooked, just in case!

YAM CHIPS

Yam 'crisps' make a delicious nibble to go with drinks, and are distinctively different from the ubiquitous potato crisp. Children love them as a snack, and they are also scrumptious served with roast beef or game birds. One of the best ways of eating yam!

1 medium sized yam, weighing about 1 lb (450 g), peeled
vegetable oil for deep-frying
salt

Cut the yam into quarters lengthwise and then slice into very fine slivers – the side of a cheese grater is excellent for doing this. Fry a handful at a time in very hot deep oil until they are puffed, crisp and golden all over. Drain on kitchen paper and keep warm whilst cooking the rest in batches. Serve as soon as possible, sprinkled with a little salt.